MY LIFE
IS NOT
FOR SALE

DR. D. K. OLUKOYA

My Life is not for sale

Dr Daniel Olukoya

My Life is not for sale
©2010.Dr Daniel Olukoya

A publication of
MOUNTAIN OF FIRE AND MIRACLES MINISTRIES
13, Olasimbo Street, off Olumo Road, Onike,
P. O. Box 2990, Sabo, Yaba, Lagos, Nigeria.

ISBN: 978-978-8424-74-1

For further information or permission contact:
Email: pasteurdanielolukoya_french@yahoo.fr
        mfmhqworldwide@mountainoffire.org

Or visit our website: www.mountainoffire.org
http://mfmbiligualbooks4evangelism.blogspot.com/

The Bible makes us to understand that the spiritual existed first before the physical. Once you understand this principle, many things become clear. The Bible also makes us to understand that things like bondage, freedom, power, anointing, etc. are spiritual items and if they are not sorted out in the spiritual realm, you are wasting your time in the physical. Real power is not in the physical world but in the spiritual world. The children of darkness understand this fact very well.

Ezekiel 13:18-19 says, "*Thus saith the Lord God; Woe to the women that sew pillows to all armholes and make kerchiefs upon the head of every stature to hunt souls. Will you hunt the souls of my people, and will ye save the souls alive that come unto you? And will you pollute me among my people for handfuls of barley and for pieces of bread, to slay the souls that should not die and to save the souls alive that should not live, by your lying to my people that hear your lies?"*

In the foregoing, we could see an exchange-taking place. The souls that are not supposed to die are being slain. They are not supposed to die but they are slain to save the souls that should not live. There are also some people that are destined to die but they look for the lives of younger persons, snuff them out and add them to themselves. They save alive the souls that should not live by lying to the people that hear their lies.

Verses 20-21 say, *"Wherefore thus saith the Lord God, Behold, I am against your pillows (pillows in original Hebrew means magic band), wherewith ye hunt the souls to make them fly (meaning that people can be initiated unconsciously). and I will tear them from your arms and will let the souls go even the souls that ye hunt to make them fly. Your kerchiefs also will I tear and deliver my people out of your hands and they shall be no more in your hand to be hunted and ye shall know that I am the LORD. "*

So, deliverance is needed to get out of their grip.

This is an interesting Scripture. Some people are using magic bands to sell the souls of men. The souls that should normally be at rest, they make them to fly. This is why when some people are asleep, they face battles. There are people after their souls, exchanging their souls for handfuls of barley and pieces of bread. Somebody goes to a herbalist and says, "I want to destroy this person," and he is asked to go and bring kolanut and goat, which would be used to snuff out the person's soul. These are powers that engage in selling souls. They exchange things. That is why I said, "My life is not for sale."

All reasonable people sell disposable things, but when a man decides to sell an indispensable item, it means that spiritual madness has crept in. Many lives are on sale. Many are being sold now and many have been sold. There is something in the spirit world known as prostitution of the soul, that is, when the soul of a person becomes a prostitute in the spirit world, all kinds of things will be happening to the soul of the person in the physical. There are people who complain that all night when they sleep, they always see spirit husband. Such people may have become prostitutes in the spirit; they have been sold off. It is very sad.

Jesus says, "What shall it profit a man if he gains the whole world and loses his soul. With what can a man make exchange for his soul? Nothing.

When the soul of a person is out on sale, it is a great problem. Jesus says, "What can you give in exchange for a soul?" In Ezekiel 13, we see people exchanging souls of men for mere pieces of bread. So, the worst enemies of men are soul traders. They hunt for souls and trade with souls.

Revelation 18:11 says, *"And the merchants of the earth shall weep and mourn over her; for no man buyeth their merchandise any more."* What is their merchandise? They are listed in Revelation 18:12-14 which says, *"The merchandise of gold and silver, and precious stones, and of pearls, and fine linen, and purple, and silk, and scarlet and thine wood, and all manner vessels of ivory, and*

*all manner vessels of most precious wood,
and of brass, and iron, and marble. And
cinnamon, and odours, and ointments, and
frankincense, and wine, and oil, and fine
flour, and wheat, and beasts, and sheep, and
horses, and chariots and slaves and souls of
men. "*

These are merchandise of soul traders.
Please, declare this to yourself, "My life is
not for sale."

Isaiah 50:1 says, *"Thus saith the Lord, Where
is the bill of your mother's divorcement,
whom I have put away? Or which of my
creditors is it to whom I have sold you?
Behold, for your iniquities have ye sold
yourselves, and for your transgressions is
your mother put away. "* That means that you
sell yourself consciously or unconsciously,

or your parents or friends can sell you off. Isaiah 52:3 also says, *"For thus saith the Lord, Ye have sold yourselves for nought; and ye shall be redeemed without money."*

When a life has been sold off, there would be destiny disorder. Several years ago, I met a sister who had this problem. Her grandmother married her off to someone in the spirit world, collected her dowry spiritually, spent it also spiritually and that grandmother was now dead. Every night, when she slept there was a short demon by her bed. She prayed and bound and loosed it to no avail. It would disappear for a while only to reappear again. When she was going to the toilet at night, it would step aside physically for her to pass. It was always there watching carefully over her anytime she was in bed. If there were other people on the bed, she would be the only person seeing the short thing. It was the guard of the husband which her grandmother married her to in the spiritual world. Five people tried to marry her but each of them ended in disaster. The one that had the least disaster was the one who drank the water of his car battery.

Please, take the following prayer points:
- Every power bargaining for my soul, die, in the name of Jesus.
- My soul, be delivered from satanic flying, in the name of Jesus.
When a life has been sold off, there would be destiny disorder. The prefix "dis" means to remove. For example, dis-ease means "remove ease." So, dis-order means a removal of order. Therefore when there is destiny dis-order, it means that the order in a destiny has been removed. Once the order is

Dr. D. K. Olukoya

removed, the destiny is as good as dead. This is the major problem of the black man. Let us look at the names of some black people in the Bible:

Hagar: an Egyptian who married Abraham.

Keturah who married Abraham.

Asenath who was Joseph's wife.

Ziporrah who was Moses' wife.

Jethro, Moses' father-in-law. He sat Moses down and taught him how to do most of what he did as a man of God.

Obab who acted as the eye of the Israelites in the wilderness. They were going to the Promised Land and did not quite know the way and this black man was their eye.

Rahab who saved the Israeli spies at Jericho.

In the book of Jeremiah, we read about a man called Ebedmelech, an Ethiopian. There was a time that Jeremiah was thrown into the

- 11 -

dungeon. It was this black man that brought him out.

In the New Testament, there is Simon of Cyrene. When Jesus was on His way to Calvary and the cross became too heavy for Him, this man carried the cross to the place of Jesus' crucifixion.

In Acts of the Apostles, we read about the Ethiopian Eunuch whom Philip preached to. When Paul was going on his missionary journey, two of the three men who laid hands on him in prayer were Lucius called Niger and Simeon of Cyrene. They were both black men.

Do you know that the gospel got to Africa before Europe? Do you know that whenever God has a major step to take in history one way or another, a black man would come along? God has always used Africa to protect, support and provide for His moves. Whenever the world was in a crisis, God brought a black man to the scene. With this background, you may now ask, what exactly is wrong with the black man? Why do white men often tell funny tales about us? Why did we blacks go through the horrifying slave trade? You cannot read the story of the slave trade without crying. Men and women were gathered and packed into the ship like sardine. There was no walking space and no toilet. When they fell sick, the only solution was to throw them inside the sea and they served as food for fishes. Why did they suffer that treatment? Why is it very difficult to find a single black nation that is now doing very well? What is responsible for the demonic and diabolical attack from hell fire to stop the black man from executing his prophetic mandate? Why should things like poverty, inferiority complex, confusion, insufficient education and civil war be rampant with blacks? It is because of destiny disorder of the individuals. When Mr. A, whose destiny is in disorder, marries a woman, whose destiny is also in disorder, they produce children who inherit destiny disorder, and the circle continues.

Please, pray like this: "I refuse to enter the dustbin of life, in the name of Jesus." There are many human beings who are already dumped into the dustbin of life and they are weeping and crying. Sometimes ago, something happened in one city in the western part of Nigeria. It was noticed that a man had a big farm and the farm was prospering. The produce from the farm was very good. But the surprising thing was that no one had ever seen any worker on that farm, yet it was the largest farm around and belonged to one old man. The man's son used to wonder about the farm. He did not understand who was planting the crops because he knew that his father was old and could not do much. As he began to cleverly study his father, he discovered that anytime he arrived at the farm, he would wash his face with some concoction. One day, the son used the concoction to wash his face and he saw the people working on the farm. They were people who had died in the village. Imagine his father's wickedness. Holding down people who were dead to serve him before they go to hell. The devil had traded their souls to the old man. When they died the man bought their souls to work in the farm. The boy screamed when he saw them. Then his father knew that he had touched the concoction. He ran after him but could not catch him because of his old age. The son disappeared into town screaming. Until now no one had seen the old man again. The farm is still there.

If you allow your soul to be sold, it is your own business. That is why when you come to the house of God, you better face your business. Do not waste time on joking with the enemy or on things that do not concern you. If you do, your disorder will multiply. It will be a major disaster if you finish reading this message without having a touch from heaven.

God has a purpose for everything He does. The fact that someone is walking about does not mean that the person is alive in the book of the Almighty. He may be moving about, breathing or going to church, but by God's reckoning, he might have died 20 years ago. God has a purpose for your life. Before you were born He has written certain things about your life. The enemy can see those things; therefore he can cause destiny disorder if he succeeds in grabbing your soul. So, the most precious material on planet earth is the soul of a man. The devil is after it, God too is after it. When Peter said to Jesus, "You cannot die like that, how can you die?" He looked at Peter and said, "The Son of man goeth as it is written of Him." Something was written about you. Is that thing in disorder now? If it is in disorder, then the soul sellers have done their worst. Sometimes ago, a woman gave birth and somebody visited her at the maternity. She gave her baby to the visitor while she went to the toilet. Shortly after, another visitor came in. As she came out of the toilet, she overheard her two visitors arguing and wondered what was happening to them. Immediately she got into the room, they became quiet. She said, "If two of you do not tell me what you were discussing, somebody will die here today." Then one of them said, "When I got here, my friend had already removed four and she wanted to remove the other three. So, all I was saying is that she should leave the other three for me." They were referring to the stars on the head of the newly born baby. This is the wickedness going on in the world.

There is no need to be alive if your life does not fulfil its divine destiny. Once your soul has been sold off, unless it is bought back, you may not be able to fulfil the destiny that the Lord has for you. For several years I thought Biology in secondary school, and in an adult education school where the youngest person in my class was 36 years old. One day, I taught about amoeba for three hours. After the lecture, I said, "Any question?" A bald headed man at the middle said he had a question. He said, "During the wedding of Amoeba who collects the dowry?" I was shocked because it means that he did not understand anything out of everything I had said for three hours. The trouble with that fellow was that he was doing the right thing at the wrong time. It is destiny disorder. He might have been interested in going to school but witches had eaten up the money of all those who would have financed his education. He might have had the brain but was unable to go to school. His destiny was in a mess.

Nahum 3:3 says, "The horsemen lifteth up both the bright sword and glittering spear: and there is a multitude of slain, and a great number of carcasses, and there is none end of their corpses, they stumble upon their corpses." What is responsible for these corpses? Verse 4 says, "Because of the multitude of the whoredom of the well-favoured harlot, the mistress of witchcrafts, that selleth nations through her whoredom and families through her witchcrafts."

SOUL TRADERS

1. Witchcraft Powers: The first major sellers of souls are witchcraft powers. We can see where their activities have led the black man today. Unfortunately, they have wangled their way into many churches. In fact, in many places today, it is mostly the witches who say, "Thus says the Lord." And many

people go to them for prayers out of ignorance. Most times in their prayer, it is only names like Olodumare, Osanobua, Chineke that would be mentioned. They do not mention the word Jesus.

When human fell in the Garden of Eden, the religion he turned to was witchcraft because he fell in rebellion. Rebellion is as the sin of witchcraft. I used to think that Taiye and Kehinde (twins) loved themselves until I saw a Kehinde who told me that she had put the life of her Taiye on the shelve, that until she married and had three or four children, her Taiye would not marry. Both of them came from the same womb but look at what witchcraft has done.

We need to be aggressive if we do not want soul traders to sell us off. A lot of people have been sold already so they do not understand what is going on. Perhaps you have been sold already and do not know.

During the slave trade, they just went to a village, captured some people and sold them off like that.

It is often said that the people who look are very many but the people who see are very few. The greatest enemy of man is not outside him, it is inside. Unless the internal defeat is registered, external defeat can never come. Unfortunately, many people who come to the house of God do not possess this ability to see. There is a need to pray the prayer of Elisha who said to his servant, "Brother, do not worry, those who are with us are more than those who are with them." The foundation of spiritual failure that the modern man is experiencing is due to spiritual blindness. A person has been sold but he does not know. A person has been thrown into jail but he does not know.

A person is wearing a three-piece suit and is studying for Ph.D. in the university but already he has been sold. Evil birds have eaten up the good seed planted in many lives. For instance, do you know the real life you are supposed to be living? Many people do not know. Have your enemies converted you to a hewer of wood and drawer of water? Look at yourself. Is your correct life dead or alive?

Have your dreams and visions, been extinguished? Are you a living dead? Is there anything that makes you to accept an inferior or disabled life as your life? Is there anything that keeps you permanently depressed and unhappy? Are you deceiving yourself by having a form of godliness but denying the power thereof? Are you the type of person who will x-ray a man or woman in the laboratory of your heart?

Perhaps you are not who you should be now. The real life of many people exist only in the dream. They count money in the dream but they are koboless in real life. They own companies only in the dream but are jobless here. They preach to thousands of people in the dream but are powerless here. They live in houses in the dream but here they have three quit notice letters.

There is something you must destroy today. You must refuse to be caged or boxed in by the enemy. You must refuse to accept the satanic substitute for your destiny. You must pray and get your unused things, and your buried Lazarus must resurrect. You must renounce the curse of powerless living. You must disallow the enemy from dulling the edge of your sword. You must disallow the enemy from closing down the factory of your life. You must refuse the call from the camp of the enemy that you should drop your weapon.

2. The second means through which souls are sold is prophetic manipulation: This is where many people make mistakes. That is why the Mountain of Fire and Miracles Ministries is a do it yourself church. It is not a place where "the man of God must pray for me" syndrome is welcomed. No. It is a "do it yourself" place. When people surrender the totality of themselves to the prophet, they are looking for destiny disorder because when God does not give a message and you ask the prophet, "What do you see?" He may give you information that is not from God. The work of a man of God is a work of high responsibility. Men of God have to be very careful.

The devil knows that people believe their pastors and would do whatever they ask them to do so he looks for his men and pushes them into the position of fake men of

God who give people demonically inspired prophecies to confuse their lives. Sometimes, parents go to the fake prophets behind their children to make their children do what they want. For example, a parent could go to such a prophet and say, "Prophet, there is one fine man coming to look for our daughter but we do not know what is wrong with the girl, she is chasing away the fine man. What we want you to do is to call her and tell her that the man is her husband." The prophet would then call the girl and say to her: "Is there anyone coming to visit you at home? That person is your husband." He says this without prayer or revelation. The sister too is not given time to pray. That way, her destiny is put in disorder.

Several years ago, a pregnant sister going to the market met a white garment prophet who said, "Thus says the Lord: Unless you bring this or that you will die with this pregnancy."

She held on to his clothes and said, "You must reverse what you have said if not, you will not leave this place." People started gathering and saying, "Sister, leave the man of God alone." She told them what he said and said they should ask him to reverse it. The people now said, "Why did you deliver such a message to the woman? Reverse it quickly." Then he said, "You will deliver safely," etc.

Several years ago, another sister came and said that a prophet in her mother's church told her that she would die, that I should pray for her and cancel it. I said, "No. You go back and tell the prophet that your pastor said: I should tell you that you will die." She went and the prophet did not last beyond the next seven days. The arrow of death went back to its sender. The devil has a way of gluing one's mind to evil prophecies. If you know that evil prophecies have been uttered against you by astrologers, unholy prophets, herbalists or that any ungodly person has foretold your future, pray this prayer point aggressively:

-Every satanic programme for my destiny, die, in the name of Jesus.

3. Joining yourself to a harlot: If you sleep with a man or woman outside marriage, you introduce disorder into your life. The Bible tells us that you become one with a sex partner. If you have gone with up to 30 to 40 men or women, it means that your life has been fragmented into many pieces. You need to pray. The destiny of Samson was reversed because of this. The way he ended up was not God's plan for his life. It was a plan of the powers of wickedness. A man who sleeps

with a married or single woman outside marriage is digging his own grave. You may think you are enjoying yourself. No. You are putting your life into disorder.

4. Contamination from the womb: This is the reason pregnant women have to be careful where they go. Drinking concoctions, attaching strange things to your dresses, paying aimless and useless visits and consumption of demonic food will cause destiny disorder.

5. Idol worship: God hates idol worship with perfect hatred. If you check your name and find something idolatrous about it, that should tell you that there is destiny disorder in place. You must cut off every linkage with that kind of thing.

6. Anger: Anger can manifest itself in several ways. It may be in shouting, slamming the door, abusive language, pounding on the tables or the ground, throwing objects at people, or destroying objects. It may be fighting, senseless argument or negative and critical comments. It may be strange look, hissing, hatred, depression or murder. Anyone with the spirit of anger already has a spirit that will put his destiny in disorder. Anger will control that person if it is not controlled. It is a powerful killer of spiritual lives. Angry people normally have retarded spiritual growth and crippled spiritual lives. They quarrel often and so they cannot pray. Angry people have bad testimony. It destroys their ability to serve the Lord and puts their destiny in disorder.

7. Household wickedness: There are many examples of this in the Bible. Jesus told us in Matthew 10:36 that the enemies of a man shall be members of his own household. Eve was used by the devil against Adam. Cain was used against Abel, Lot against Abraham and Jacob against Esau. Joseph's brethren dealt with him. Miriam, Moses' sister who took Moses out of the river was against him.

Absalom overthrew his father. Judas Iscariot one of Jesus' 12 disciples was household wickedness to Jesus.
We need to pray, not the type of prayer the enemy will hear and rejoice. The first thing we need to do is to repent before the Lord of anything that has given the enemy the ground to sell our souls or tamper with our lives. We need to ask God to forgive us so that we can start moving forward. After asking for forgiveness, we will move on and

identify the disorder, and then call God into our situation. It will be a tragedy after reading this message you do not receive the touch of God. The Bible says, "The Son of man goeth as it is written." Are you going as God has written of you, or you are going as your enemy has written? Or are you going according to verdict of witchcraft? You have the opportunity to ask God to forgive you.

If you are reading this and you are yet to surrender to Jesus, you better do so quickly before you move into the prayer section. Otherwise you cannot introduce order into your life. If you want to surrender your life to Jesus, pray this prayer: "Lord Jesus, I come before you and confess my sins. Forgive me, O Lord, and cleanse me with your precious blood. Come into my life now. Take control of my life, in Jesus' name. Amen."

PRAYER POINTS

1. O Lord, let my prayer arrow bring results, in Jesus' name.
2. (Use your right hand to cover your two eyes as you pray this prayer with faith): Oh Lord, reveal hidden things to me that will move me forward, in the name of Jesus.
3. Every power that has refused to allow my star to operate, die, in Jesus' name.
4. I recover my stolen stars by fire, in the name of Jesus.
5. I recover my stolen stars by thunder, in the name of Jesus.
6. I reject every evil prophecy, in the name of Jesus.

ABOUT D. K. OLUKOYA

Dr. D. K. Olukoya is the General Overseer of the Mountain of Fire and Miracles Ministries and the Battle Cry Ministries. He holds a First Class Honours Degree in Microbiology from the University of Lagos, Nigeria and a Ph.D. in Molecular Genetics from the University of Reading, United Kingdom. As a researcher, he has over eighty scientific publications to his credit. Anointed by God, Dr. Olukoya is a teacher, prophet, evangelist and preacher of the word. His life and that of his wife, Shade and their son, Elijah Toluwani, are living proofs that all power belongs to God.

ABOUT MOUNTAIN OF FIRE AND MIRACLES MINISTRIES

Mountain of Fire and Miracles Ministries, is a ministry devoted to the revival of apostolic signs, Holy Ghost fireworks and the unlimited demonstration of the power of God to deliver to the uttermost. Absolute holiness within and without, as the greatest spiritual insecticide, and a condition for heaven is taught openly. MFM is a do-it-yourself Gospel Ministry, where your hands are trained to wage war and your fingers to fight.

A brief history of Mountain of Fire and Miracles Ministries Incorporated
The Mountain of Fire and Miracles was founded in 1989.

The first meeting was held at the home of Dr. D. K Olukoya and had 24 persons in attendance. The Church later moved to No. 60, Old Yaba Road, Lagos, and then to the present International Headquarters, site on 24th April, 1994. The Mountain of Fire and Miracles Ministries' Headquarters is the largest single Christian congregation in Africa, with attendance of over 200,000 in single meetings. Mountain of Fire and Miracles Ministries is a full gospel ministry devoted to the revival of apostolic signs, Holy Ghost fireworks and the unlimited demonstration of the power of God to deliver to the uttermost. Absolute holiness, within and without, as the greatest spiritual insecticide and a pre-requisite for heaven is taught openly. MFM is a do-it-yourself Gospel ministry, where your hands are trained to wage war and your fingers to do battle.

www.ingramcontent.com/pod-product-compliance
Lightning Source LLC
Chambersburg PA
CBHW070752050426
42449CB00010B/2444